Do Kangaroos Swim?

Written and Illustrated by Keith L. Huff
Color by Joshua Schiller

Next
Page
Publishers
L.L.C.
Louisville, Kentucky

To All My Friends

Thanks to Hank, Brian, Grace and Josh

Published by

Next Page Publishers LLC
Louisville, Kentucky

Do Kangaroos Swim? TM
By Keith L. Huff

Next Page Publisher books may be purchased for educational, business, or sales promotional use. For more information email **klhuff@nextpagepublishers.com**

FIRST EDITION
ISBN: 9781718045491

Designed by Keith L. Huff & Josh Schiller

Editors: Keith L. Huff

Visit us on the web at **https://www.nextpagepublishers.com**

Do Kangaroos Swim?

DID YOU KNOW!

Australia is a Latin word meaning "Southern Land."

Humans first inhabited Australia 48,000 years ago.

The boomerang is a weapon used by Australian Aborigines for hunting. This curved flat piece of wood, when thrown, will return to the thrower.

Australia has a lot of kangaroos. But, did you know
that there are over 60 types of Kangaroos in Australia?

Like red kangaroos,

tree kangaroos,

and there's even a kangaroo rat!

Australia also has wallaby's, which is like a kangaroo but smaller.

Kangaroos can jump very long distances. The Red kangaroo can leap 6 feet in the air with a distance of 25 feet long!

But what about swimming?

YES! Kangaroos can swim and are pretty good.

They mainly swim to evade predators like the Tasmanian Devil.

A special kangaroo named Joey loves to swim.

Joey's a grey kangaroo, which are much smaller then red kangaroos.

Everyday Joey swims by himself, because none of the other kangaroos like to swim for fun.

One day, Joey's mother told him they had to move away to another part of Australia.

"Do I still get to swim?" he asked.

"Of course. Maybe you could even find friends that like to swim, "she assured him.

"Oh boy!" Joey cried.

Joey and his mother moved to Uluru, a desert area of Australia.

This is a very hot and dry area with very little water.

Joey was sad. In this part of Australia there are no kangaroos, only black wallabies that are not very friendly.

One day as Joey was daydreaming about swimming, he heard a noise beyond a thicket of bushes.

The noise was coming from a snake that intends on hurting a baby turtle.

As the snake was about to strike the baby turtle, he fell flat to the ground.

Joey had jumped with all his might to pin down the slimy serpent.

The snake slithered away never to return.

"Are you ok?" Joey asked.

"Yeah, I'm Ok," the turtle said poking his head out of his shell.

"Who are you"? Joey asked

"I'm Hank."

"I'm Joey, What Type of turtle are you?"

"Snapping turtle, and you, You're a grey kangaroo. You're not from around here."

"Nope."

"Gee thanks for saving me," Hank said. "Hey, do you swim?"

"Yes, I love swimming," Joey said with such enthusiasm he nearly fell to the ground.

"Me too!"

"Too bad there's no place to swim," Joey said sadly.

"Yeah there is!" Hank replied.

"Really! Where?" Joey asked standing tall.

Hank leads Joey into a wide opening of the mountain.

A pond for swimming is nestled at the heart of the mountain.

Hank and Joey become best friends as they swim in the cool waters of Uluru.

For the first time since arriving at his new home, Joey was happy.

He had found a new friend whom he could share his passion of swimming with.

THE
END

Colorist

Joshua Schiller operates Fishwood Inn at http://www.fishwoodinn.com.

Joshua is the co-author and illustrator of the children's book *The Story of Little Pickle*.

Joshua also works in clay sculpting. His work has been featured in the short film *For Sale By Owner*.